BRITAIN IN PICTURES
THE BRITISH PEOPLE IN PICTURES

THE CONSERVATIVE PARTY

THE DUKE OF WELLINGTON AND SIR ROBERT PEEL
Oil painting by Franz Xaver Winterhalter, 1851

THE
CONSERVATIVE PARTY

NIGEL BIRCH

WITH
4 PLATES IN COLOUR
AND
21 ILLUSTRATIONS IN
BLACK & WHITE

COLLINS · 14 ST. JAMES'S PLACE · LONDON
MCMXLIX

PRODUCED BY
ADPRINT LIMITED LONDON

PRINTED IN GREAT BRITAIN BY
CLARKE & SHERWELL LTD NORTHAMPTON
ON MELLOTEX BOOK PAPER MADE BY
TULLIS RUSSELL & CO LTD MARKINCH SCOTLAND

LIST OF ILLUSTRATIONS

PLATES IN COLOUR

BLACK AND WHITE ILLUSTRATIONS

*The Editor is most grateful to all those who have so kindly helped in the selection of illustrations,
especially to officials of the various public Museums, Libraries and Galleries, and to all others
who have generously allowed pictures and MSS. to be reproduced*

PART I

HISTORY OF THE PARTY UP TO 1945

BEGINNINGS

THE word Conservative was first used as a party name by the supporters of Sir Robert Peel soon after the Reform Bill of 1832. The men who adopted it were the successors in the direct line of the old Tory Party, and the Tory name is far from dead to-day. The needs of the sub-editor and the malice of our opponents would in any case keep it alive but it is significant that the left wing of the Conservative Party chose the name Tory Reform during the war and that the Party's weekly journal, formerly called *The Onlooker*, was recently given the more robust title of *Tory Challenge*. "Tory" (originally meaning an Irish bandit) was shouted about the year 1678 at the Cavaliers as a term of execration and abuse by Titus Oates, the most venomous perjurer recorded in British history. The Kaiser called our 1914 regular Army "a contemptible little Army," and the survivors were proud to call themselves "Old Contemptibles." In the same way the statesmen of the Right in the reign of Charles II and those that came after were and are content to bear a name given them by the hatred of their enemies.

The Tory Party under other names is as old as party itself. The first germs of party in Britain can be dated from the wedding of Henry VIII and Anne Boleyn which signalised our disunion from Catholic Europe and the setting-up of a National Church. The Anglican Church Settlement, as it was worked out under Queen Elizabeth, was itself eminently conservative and the Conservatives of the day were those who approved it and had no wish either to go back to Rome or on to Geneva. The prophet of the new Church was the gentle and saintly Hooker whose theme was the *Respublica Christiana*, the identity of Church and nation, the religious basis of the State and the perfect harmony of the Elizabethan system both with the laws of scripture and the laws of reason. Hooker stands high in the spiritual lineage of the Tory Party, and for much of their history the Tories have been the Church party. Though exclusive claims have long been given up and the Party has often been led by Nonconformists, from

7

Harley in the reign of Queen Anne to Bonar Law and the Chamberlains in our own day, the idea of the religious basis of society and of the fundamental unity of all Christian men in whatever way they worship God has not been abandoned. As Burke wrote, "We know and we feel inwardly that religion is the basis of civil society and the source of all good and all comfort." The vision has never faded, and under the threat of a Marxist anti-Church the bonds that unite all Christian men are increasingly known to be of more importance than the schisms which divide them.

But the idea of unity in diversity did not prevail during the seventeenth century. The lack of understanding of Britain shown by the early Stuarts and their attempt to prolong the Tudor system in face of the claims of Parliament and growing religious division ended in civil war. Few Cavaliers upheld the doctrine of divine right—as a doctrine it only claimed any number of adherents after the execution of Charles I—fewer still sympathised with the pretensions of Archbishop Laud; all the earlier reforms were supported by Cavaliers; Strafford refused to pay his share of the forced loan in 1626 and joined in forcing the Petition of Right upon the King; Falkland and Hyde supported the Triennial Act and joined in abolishing the Star Chamber, the Council of Wales and the Court of High Commission. What the Cavaliers were not prepared to see was the disruption of the Church, the overthrow of the Constitution, and the abolition of the Monarchy and House of Lords. They took up arms in 1642 with heavy hearts, for the Church rather than the bishops, the Constitution rather than the Ministers and the Crown rather than the King. They wanted reform but not revolution. Monarchy, a national Church and the House of Lords are to-day, three hundred years after they fought, still essential parts of our national life. What was destroyed by the war, and brought back at the Restoration, was in accord with the permanent interests and wishes of the nation.

The Commonwealth with its persecutions and confiscations and the rule of the Major-Generals had two permanent effects on the Tory Party. Army rule made the Party for long opponents of any standing army, and has still left them adherents of the blue-water school with a strong disbelief in the use for this country of Continental warfare with mass armies; and secondly the memory of having once been a hunted minority has made them fundamentally pacific, abhorrers of force, with an acute sense of time's revenges. Sir Hartley Shawcross's boast "We are the masters now" would not have fallen from Tory lips. Perhaps for this reason at the Restoration in 1660, under the wise guidance of Clarendon, great moderation was shown. In spite of the passions aroused by the Civil War and its aftermath only ten regicides were executed and some twenty excluded from pardon. Mercy to political opponents has never been a characteristic of the left and it has altogether gone out of fashion in the century of the Common Man.

8

THE EIGHTEENTH CENTURY

If the Restoration of the Stuarts was a Tory triumph, the death in 1714 of Queen Anne, the last Stuart monarch, marked the beginning of a period of defeat and division which kept the Party out of power for nearly fifty years. The ability of Bolingbroke had brought the War of the Spanish Succession to an end and concluded the Peace of Utrecht, a necessary though unscrupulous transaction, but his ambition and lack of judgment led most of the Party into a policy of religious intolerance and some of the Party into the Jacobite camp. His flight to the Court of the Pretender soon after the arrival in England of George I was enough to convince the first two monarchs of the House of Hanover that the Tories were not to be trusted. Walpole could always rely on provoking William Shippen, the leader of the Jacobite wing in the Commons, into saying something sufficiently indiscreet to be unpleasing to Hanoverian ears; thus "Honest"

Shippen performed something of the same service for the Whigs now rendered by Sir Waldron Smithers, with his extreme *laissez-faire* views, to Mr. Herbert Morrison. Bolingbroke having quarrelled with the Pretender was permitted to return to England, though not to sit in the House of Lords again, and once back he started the writing of that long series of books and pamphlets in which he sought to undo the harm he had done to his party, and to give it a new faith and mission. He sought to purge it of Jacobitism and religious intolerance, to preach a monarchy broad-based on the popular will, to advocate shorter parliaments and the exclusion of place-men from Parliament, to reduce the influence of the peerage on elections and to uphold the landed interest against the power of the new moneyed men from the towns. His preaching fell on attentive ears, for during their long period of power the Whigs were corrupt, unfriendly to the landed interest, excessively favourable to the moneyed classes, and they built up a strong and exclusive power based on the sharing of the spoils of office among the great Revolution families. While the Whigs were triumphant and aristocratic the Tories were depressed and small-squireish.

On the other hand, the Tories were the popular party and almost certainly enjoyed the support of a majority of the nation, which prevented the Whigs doing anything which did extreme violence to fundamental Tory beliefs. Disraeli described the great Whig houses as the Venetian Oligarchy, and from this time can be traced the Tory dislike of oligarchy or exclusive power whether wielded by an aristocracy of birth, of labour or of industry. From this time too can be traced that distrust—so evident to-day—of extended Government patronage; for the eighteenth-century agitation against place-men transposed into a contemporary key is, in essence, the agitation against "jobs for the boys."

On the accession of George III, who "gloried in the name of Briton," the Court became reconciled with the Tories and the Tories with the Court. Jacobitism was no longer more than a sentiment. Dr. Johnson, the highest of Tories, who always referred to the Hanoverian succession as "the usurpation" and used to "roar with prodigious violence" against George II, was a loyal and devoted subject of George III. Unfortunately, the new King ascended the throne determined to break the system of cabinet government built up by the Whigs and to restore personal rule through non-party Governments of Tories, Whigs, Chathamites and King's Friends, and he made a monumental mess of it. The King himself lacked the ability to rule, and the hotchpotch of incompatibilities raked together to form Governments (one such Government was described by Burke as "a tessellated pavement without cement") showed all the muddle, friction and lack of decision characteristic of coalition Governments. The experiment ended with the loss of the American colonies and the unprincipled coalition between Fox and North. From these days may be dated the Conservative dislike of coalitions.

WILLIAM PITT, 1759-1806
Water colour by James Gillray

THE REVIVAL UNDER PITT

The country had had enough, and the younger Pitt was called to power
in 1783 at twenty-four years of age. He was in power for nineteen out of
the next twenty-three years, and his rise was the start of a period of Tory
predominance which did not end until 1830. It was his task to reconcile
the Tory idea of monarchism with Whig parliamentarianism, to restore
the cabinet system of government and to initiate a series of Conservative
reforms. He reorganised the financial system of the country (the theme of
seventeen budget speeches was "let us look our difficulties in the face"),
he remoulded the Governments of India and Canada, he supported the
Tory Wilberforce in his campaign against the slave trade (ultimately to
be crowned with success after one of the longest and most skilful campaigns
of parliamentary agitation in British history), he proposed reforms in the

franchise and initiated a policy of conciliation in Ireland. The first ten years of his Ministry were years of peace and bore good fruit, and his zeal and competence gave great promise for the future, particularly if the King's scruples on Catholic emancipation could be broken down; but these hopes were blighted by the coming of the French Revolutionary Wars, which were fought with but one short break from 1793 till 1815.

In the long war which ended on the field of Waterloo, during which we were three times left alone in face of the overwhelming military ascendancy of the enemy, the Tory Party, taught by Burke, learnt to take pride in the defence of the constitutional settlement which followed the Revolution of 1688. The Party stood for parliamentary government and against the savagery of the Jacobins and the despotism of Napoleon. Above all, Britain fought to prevent the domination of the Continent by a single dictator in the same way as she fought Louis XIV, William II of Germany and Adolf Hitler. In 1794 Burke, the major prophet of Conservatism, left his seat near Fox and Sheridan and crossed the floor of the House of Commons to support Pitt. He had advocated with all his power and persuasiveness conciliation with America, toleration in Ireland, the end of corruption in English politics and the purging of the Indian administration of tyranny and fraud, and on the same principles he denounced the cruelties of the Jacobins and the subversive activities of their English sympathisers

WILLIAM WILBERFORCE, 1759-1833
Unfinished oil painting by Sir Thomas Lawrence

VISCOUNT CASTLEREAGH, 1769-1822
Oil painting by Sir Thomas Lawrence

in words which to-day, a hundred and fifty years after they were spoken,
are still incandescent. When this country is in opposition to a tyranny of
the right, sympathisers with the tyrant will be few—they were virtually
non-existent in the First and Second World Wars—but when the country
is in opposition to a tyranny of the Left there is sure to be a fifth column or,
perhaps more accurately, there are sure to be "fellow travellers." During
the Napoleonic Wars our "fellow travellers" were numerous and violent,
and such men as Tom Paine, Joseph Priestley and Richard Price welcomed
the Revolution with enthusiasm and looked to the speedy establishment
of a secular republic in Britain. A Conservative country, disgusted by
the September massacres, had no sympathy with those who sought to
weaken their own country and strengthen a foreign one with which we
were at war. The measures of repression which were taken were

undoubtedly approved by the country as a whole—as have been the much milder ones taken recently by Mr. Attlee against those who see nothing wrong in slave labour camps in Siberia and welcomed the judicial murder of Petkov—but they were harsh and were prolonged and intensified after the war. That repression is no substitute for necessary reform and that enthusiasts should be gently handled are the lessons which the Conservative Party learnt from the bitter years that followed Waterloo.

Castlereagh, who, as War Minister, had supported Wellington's Peninsular campaign, against the attacks of the Whigs, negotiated the peace settlement at the Congress of Vienna. In our own day the memory of Castlereagh has been rehabilitated, but until recently he was invariably an object of abuse by historians of the Left. In this generation we have some experience of peace settlements and attempted peace settlements and we are less inclined than our fathers to scoff at one which prevented a general European war for ninety-nine years.

The triumph over Napoleon gave the Tories another fifteen years in office, but they were distressful years full of new problems, and the Party was getting out of touch with the new middle class to whom power would soon fall. The country's economy, as was inevitable after a great war, was out of balance; the new and unsolved problems caused by the Industrial Revolution were piling up and the population was beginning to grow fast. How life was to be made tolerable for forty millions in a country where it had been hard for seven millions to live before was the problem which the century would have to solve. There was unemployment and there were riots—and riots were serious in a country which was without police until Sir Robert Peel started them in London in 1829, where they have been affectionately known as "Bobbies" ever since.

Some reforms had been carried out during the war, but the years 1815-22 were barren years. After 1822 fears of revolution began to subside and some useful work was done, including first steps in Trade Union legislation in 1824 and 1825, the abolition of the death penalty for many minor offences, a considerable liberalising of our economy (the Whigs were then the more protectionist party) and, much to Wellington's annoyance, the recognition of the revolted South American colonies of Spain. To have defeated Napoleon, to have obstructed the less creditable designs of Metternich, to have carried out measures to liberalise our economy and at any rate some social reforms and to have avoided a revolution are claims to the gratitude of posterity not altogether to be disregarded; but the Tories had been in power too long and they were broken by their own divisions on Catholic emancipation and parliamentary reform. Had they lived, it is possible that the brilliance of Canning (a strong supporter of Catholic claims) and the good nature of Lord Liverpool might have got the Party over both hurdles; but their deaths left Wellington in a dominant position, and though, after Marlborough, the greatest soldier ever bred in this

14

GEORGE CANNING, 1770-1827
Oil painting by Sir Thomas Lawrence.

country, he was not a good politician. "The party," he said, "what is the
meaning of a party if they don't follow their leaders? Damn 'em, let 'em
go." Damn 'em, chuck 'em out, is Mr. Herbert Morrison's up-to-the-
minute amendment, but neither accords with the Conservative ideal of
leadership by consent. In 1829 Wellington and Peel were finally forced by
the threat of violence to concede Catholic emancipation, which they should
long since have freely granted. Another retreat on parliamentary reform
immediately after this fiasco was too much and the Party fell from power
in 1830. In 1832 Lord Grey secured the passage of his Reform Bill.

At the General Election of 1833 only 149 Tories were returned. "We have buried the Tories," wrote Parkes, the Radical organiser of Birmingham, "and if the Whigs will not do right the sexton must be called out again." The sentiment and even the words are curiously familiar—but it was the Tories who survived and it was the Whigs for whom the sexton was to be called out.

In retrospect it is strange that the Reform Bill of 1832 should have created such jubilation among Radicals, for what it did was to give the vote to one household in six—to all the landlords and half the middle class. Moreover, and this was a point that Tories made the most of, the Bill had the effect of disfranchising a large number of working men who, under an erratic electoral system inherited from a remote past, had the right to vote in certain popular constituencies such as Westminster. Nevertheless, the break with the past was a sharp one and if the Tories were to play their part in the future much dead wood must be cut away. There would be no place in the years to come for the monopoly of power by an exclusive aristocracy or an exclusive Church.

The work of re-creating the Party was started by Peel, whose task it was to accommodate Toryism to the Britain of the Reform Bill, that is to say to a Britain where power resided in the middle class. There were two obvious needs—a restatement of policy and a reorganisation of the Party. What Peel did was to issue the Tamworth Manifesto and to set up a central party organisation. Though the circumstances are not strictly comparable, there is an obvious parallel between what he did in 1834 and the issue of the Industrial Charter and the appointment of Lord Woolton to the Conservative Central Office after the election of 1945.

When the Tamworth Manifesto was issued all that was remembered of the Party was that it had been in opposition to the Reform Bill. Peel, the son of a cotton-spinner, understood the middle-class mind and sympathised with the sufferings of the poor much more than he understood and sympathised with many of his own party, and he also understood the economic needs of the trading and financial community far better than most Tories or most Whigs. He was therefore well fitted for the task of setting out a middle-class policy. The Manifesto accepted the Reform Bill as irrevocable and proposed a careful review of our institutions and a number of specific measures including municipal reform, the opening of medical and legal education to Nonconformists, the commutation of tithes and so on. The Manifesto did wonders in the constituencies, and though the Conservatives did not command a majority at the General Election of 1835 they came back 250 strong with an actual majority of English seats.

The Whig Government of Lord Melbourne (it was under his Government that the Tolpuddle "Martyrs" were transported) carried out a number

'PUNCH'S MONUMENT TO PEEL'
Drawing by John Leech, July 1850

of middle-class reforms much in accord with the ideas of the Manifesto and imposed the new Poor Law (the harshness of which extreme Radicals and Tories combined to oppose) but did little or nothing for the working man. The agitation for shorter hours for women and children in the textile industry and for Government inspection of factories, for the prohibition of work by women and young boys in mines, and for the care of destitute

17

children was led by Lord Shaftesbury and his evangelical Tory friends Oastler and Sadler. Their work was to bear fruit in the years to come. It was no accident that the fight for better conditions for working men was led by Tories. The rising class of manufacturers, able, energetic men but hard, skin-flint employers, were almost to a man Liberals or Radicals with an unshakable faith in the merits of *laissez-faire* and a strong hostility to the landed interest and often to the Church.

The Whigs after the triumph of the Reform Bill soon sank in lethargy and division. In the election of 1841 Peel was returned with a comfortable majority. He started to carry out a vigorous programme of financial, economic and social reform. In the Budget of 1841 import duties were reduced on 750 articles and as a set-off an income tax on incomes of £150 per annum and over was re-introduced at the conservative rate of 7*d.* in the £, with the prospect of its abolition in five years' time. A Coal Regulation Act (opposed by Bright) was passed which prohibited the employment of women and young boys in mines, and the Bank Charter Act of 1844 laid down the principles on which the Bank of England was conducted until 1931. Everything pointed to a generation of power for the Tories, when the Party was shattered by the Corn Law crisis of 1846. The abolition of the Corn Laws was the culmination of the long campaign of agitation by the Anti-Corn-Law League against all taxes or prohibitions on the import of wheat. Cobden and Bright were the leaders, and besides putting forward a closely reasoned case they used language of great violence to inflame popular passion. Cobden denounced the Corn Law as "a law that had been baptised in blood, begotten in violence and injustice and perpetuated at the expense of the tears and groans of the people." Peel finally became intellectually convinced by the repealers' case and (assisted by Wellington in the Lords who followed his usual principle "the Queen's Government must be supported") forced through the abolition of the Corn Laws.

The Tory opposition to the abolition of the Corn Laws was led by Disraeli, who had been elected to Parliament in 1837. He attacked Peel with bitter sarcasm and invective as a turncoat and a betrayer of the landed interest. What the anti-repealers objected to was not so much the repeal of the duty as that agriculture was being put on the same level as the production of candlesticks or rope and no longer recognised as a way of life, the prosperity and stability of which were a matter of permanent interest to the country. The fears of the opponents of repeal were not realised until the late 1870's, when the spread of railways in the New World brought in a flood of cheaply produced corn and caused a long and bitter agricultural depression in the country. The memory of the Corn Law agitation, however, persisted and though unsuccessful efforts were made in the elections of 1906 and 1923, it was not till 1931 that the country would agree to any form of agricultural protection.

THE DISRAELI CABINET, 1874 - 1880

Oil painting by Charles Mercier

Peel resigned in 1846, taking with him a personal following of one hundred and twenty so-called Peelites and leaving the rump of the Tory Party under the leadership of Lord Derby (the Rupert of debate) and Disraeli. The Peelites, the most distinguished of whom was Gladstone, an ardent Tory in his youth, went the way of all centre parties in England, and after the death of Peel in 1850 they gradually dissolved, the bulk of them joining the Liberal Party. The Conservative Party did not again enjoy a clear majority until 1874.

The abolition of the Corn Laws in 1846 marked the triumph of *laissez-faire*. But next year an Act ultimately more significant was passed which attacked the root principles of *laissez-faire*. In 1847 the Ten Hours Act, limiting the working hours of all persons under 18 years of age and of women in the textile industry, was brought in by Fielden and got through the Commons by a combination of Tories and Old Whigs. The bulk of the Peelites and their Radical allies in the Corn Law fight, including Cobden and Bright, voted against the Bill which Bright described as "miserable legislation on principles false and mischievous." When the Lords made no trouble over the bill the outraged *Economist* published an article entitled "The Lords leagued with the Commons to prohibit Industry." The Free Trade *laissez-faire* school undoubtedly voted against the bill with a good conscience, on principle and not as a matter of expediency. They believed that complete freedom would bring peace and prosperity and that nothing else would. To a Tory it seems that setting up ideas, whether they are *laissez-faire* ideas or Socialist ideas, and worshipping them as idols is apt to lead to actions devoid of both sense and humanity. In the event, the reign of pure *laissez-faire* was short; the weight of the State, which could hardly be felt in the factories, the mines, the ships and the schools in 1830, was sensible by 1870 and strong by 1880.

THE RISE OF DISRAELI

The break-up of the Conservative Party in 1846 brought in a period of party confusion with power resting in the main with various coalitions of Peelites and Liberals, one of which blundered into the Crimean War. It was the age of the Whig Lord Palmerston's strength and popularity: and in everything, except an incurable itch to interfere with the internal affairs of foreign nations, Lord Palmerston was a Tory—hence the political calm. It was during this time that Disraeli built up his position with the nation, and in the Party, by his genius and unremitting labour. Disraeli saw that, in the future, Toryism must be popular Toryism or it would be nothing. He had done much in his speeches, and novels, to rouse interest in the "Condition of the People" question, and to identify himself with the interests and sufferings of the poor, and he had taken every opportunity in

Parliament to force through remedial social legislation, but he also saw that as well as looking after their interests it was necessary to touch the emotions of the people by appealing to the greatness of the country of which they were a part and the splendour of her Imperial traditions. He knew that a reform of the franchise was bound to come, and it was his strength with his party which enabled him to carry through his Electoral Reform Bill in 1867. A strong agitation had been carried on in the country in favour of a further extension of the franchise. The Whigs were divided on the issue and had resigned, and Lord Derby and Disraeli were in office, though in a minority, in the House of Commons. Disraeli was determined that the mistakes of 1832 should not be repeated, that a radical measure of reform should be carried and that the Conservatives should do it. His Bill, as finally amended, granted household franchise in the towns, thus decisively removing ultimate power from the middle class and giving it to the working classes. It was not merely a question of political tactics; Disraeli had a profound belief that democracy is Tory, and events have not proved him wrong.

The middle-class Reform Bill of 1832 gave the Whigs nine years of office followed by a major Tory victory. The Reform Bill of 1867 gave six years of office to the Liberals, and the Tories another six. The introduction of the secret ballot and the subsequent extension of the household franchise to the counties, which was brought in by the Liberals in 1884, eclipsed the Tories for six months and then put them in power for seventeen of the next twenty years. The next great extension of the franchise in 1918 put the Conservatives in effective power for twenty-four of the next twenty-seven years. There were other factors at work, no doubt, but it can hardly be doubted that Disraeli's maxim "trust the people" has proved a wise one for Conservatives.

In 1874 Disraeli was returned to power with the first clear Conservative majority since the election of 1841. He was in his seventieth year. Perhaps his exclusion from power during the best years of his life was a judgment on him for his treatment of Peel in 1846, but it was a misfortune for the country, which had to wait too long for the measures which he brought in in 1874-80. Disraeli's maxim had been "Pure air, pure water, the inspection of unhealthy habitations and the prevention of the adulteration of food," a policy denounced by the Liberals as "a policy of sewage." The measures taken included another Factory Act and important Public Health and Food and Drug Acts, which are the foundations of public health administration to-day. These Bills were followed by the Artisans' Dwellings Act (the first slum-clearance Act in our history), a useful Bill to ensure the adoption of sound insurance principles by Friendly Societies, a Merchant Shipping Act for the safety and protection of seamen, and the Compulsory Education Act of 1876. The Employers and Workmen Act of 1875 and the Conspiracy Act of the same year recognised in their entirety the freedom of contract and the right of collective bargaining, wise and timely measures of pacification which rank in our history with the Ten Hours Bill of 1847. A vote of thanks to the Government for their help to trade unions was passed at the Trades Union Congress in 1875. Mr. Alexander Macdonald, an early type of Labour Member (he called himself "Liberal and Labour"), not unjustly said in 1879: "The Conservatives have done more for the working classes in five years than the Liberals in fifty."

In foreign and Imperial affairs these years saw the proclamation of the Queen as Empress of India, a title abandoned in 1948, the acquisition of the Suez Canal shares, and the blocking of Russian ambitions in the Balkans and the Near East at the Congress of Berlin in 1878. As a set-off to these foreign and domestic services, the agricultural depression, predicted in 1846 when the Corn Laws were abolished, descended on the country and in addition, Mr. Gladstone came out of his retirement and in speeches and pamphlets of flaming eloquence roused the country with his denunciations of Turkish atrocities in Bulgaria. The Conservatives lost the election of 1880 and Disraeli, after completing his last political novel at the age of 75, died in 1881 full of years and honours.

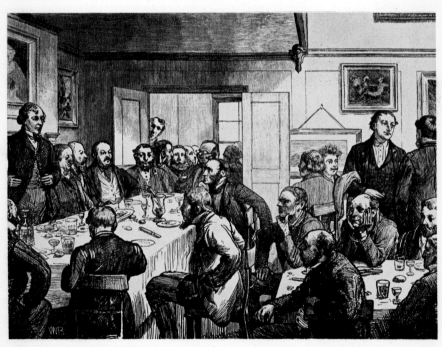

DISRAELI AT A MARKET ORDINARY AT AYLESBURY AT ELECTION TIME
Engraving from the *Illustrated London News*, February, 1874

21

LORD SALISBURY, 1830-1903
Original cartoon by Spy

For the bulk of the period between the elections of 1880 and 1906 the Conservatives were in power. By declaring for Home Rule for Ireland, Gladstone split the Liberal Party as Peel had split the Tory Party over the Corn Laws forty years before. The part played by the Peelites in 1846 was played by the Liberal Unionists (78 strong at the General Election of 1886) led by Joseph Chamberlain, who formed an alliance with the Conservatives which has lasted ever since. The Liberal Unionists are no longer a separate entity but the name Unionist survives in the official title of the Party and is still used in preference to Conservative in Scotland and in Northern Ireland. Those who objected to Home Rule not only hated the division of the United Kingdom but they feared the damage that might be caused to Britain in war by a neutral or hostile Ireland on her flank, and they were not prepared to betray their Protestant allies in Ulster. Though the Liberal Party fought almost to the last to include Ulster in the Irish Free State, Ulster was not betrayed in the settlement after the First World War and still remains part of the United Kingdom.

From the death of Disraeli till near his own death in 1903 Lord Salisbury led the Conservative Party. Unlike Peel and Disraeli he was not on the left of his party — he did not skirmish in front of it. He was a man devout yet profoundly sceptical, far-seeing and courageous, caring more for administration than legislation and always determined to preserve the unity, the safety and the strength of his country. One of his sayings could have been studied with advantage by those responsible for our Palestine policy. "In foreign affairs the choice of a policy is as a rule of less importance than the methods by which it is pursued." A hard saying perhaps, but what dangers and humiliations we should have been spared if the Socialists had reflected on it and understood it before they undertook to solve the problem of the Arabs and the Jews! If the balance of the Conservative Party was to be preserved and it was to fulfil its mission under a leader of the right, strong personalities were needed on the left of the party and they were found in Lord

LORD RANDOLPH CHURCHILL 1849-1894
Cartoon by Spy from *Vanity Fair*

23

Randolph Churchill during the first part of this period and in Mr. Joseph Chamberlain in the second. Lord Randolph, a brilliant demagogue, led what might be described as the "Tory Reform" movement of his day. He had a profound confidence in the sanity, patriotism and conservatism of the British working man, and some words of his which startled at the time have a topical ring to-day. "If you want to gain the confidence of the working classes, let them have a share and a large share—a real share and not a sham share—in your party councils and your party Government."

Joseph Chamberlain, who started politics as an extreme Radical, had two passions—the unity and development of the Empire, and social reform. During his eight years at the Colonial Office he attacked the problems of the Empire with a fire and energy which had not been seen before, and he was responsible for calling together the first Imperial Conference in 1897. As Mayor of Birmingham he had been a pioneer in municipal enterprise in housing and health and in the supply of water, gas and electricity. In Parliament he worked for many causes, including workmen's compensation, education, local-government reform and old-age pensions. The first Workmen's Compensation Act of 1897, the Act setting up County Councils in 1888 and the Education Act of 1902 which put the National system of voluntary and provided schools under Local Education Authorities and gave power to provide secondary and technical schools were all, in large part, due to his efforts.

Joseph Chamberlain's passion for the Empire was a contributory cause of the loss of the Election in 1906. He saw that Imperial Preference was essential if his plans for the welding together of the Empire were to be carried out, and Imperial Preference was not consistent with Free Trade dogma. Thus the whole question of Protection versus Free Trade was raised once again. To-day when import and export licences, bulk purchase and State trading are more important obstacles to the freedom of trade than tariffs, the controversy in its old form has lost much of its meaning, but up till the Second World War it was a burning political issue. Protectionists believed first in Imperial Preference. Imperial Preference has recently become part of Socialist policy, and even Liberal opposition to it is much less strong than it was. Secondly, protectionists believed that to accept Free Trade as an unalterable doctrine, to accept it *de fide*, was to adopt a policy of unilateral disarmament and would weaken our international bargaining power. The last major triumph of Free Trade was Cobden's French treaty in 1860. Since then there has been a general tendency for tariffs to rise throughout the world and it is difficult to believe that tying our own hands did anything to slow down the process. Thirdly, they believed that Protection could do something to mitigate unemployment. Until the 1930's the classical school of economists denied that Protection could under any circumstances do anything to alleviate unemployment but this position was abandoned by Keynes in his *General*

JOSEPH CHAMBERLAIN, 1836-1914
Ink drawing by Phil May

Theory published in 1936 and is no longer held by any school of thought in the old dogmatic form. The protectionists therefore had much reason on their side but some of the Party were still free-traders and more held, and held rightly, that the country was not ready to reverse the Free Trade policy so long pursued. Balfour, who had taken over the leadership when Salisbury retired, was haunted by the memory of the split in the Party over the Corn Laws in 1846 and was determined not to play the part of Peel, so he temporised and sought refuge in ambiguity. The Party therefore faced the General Election of 1906 divided among themselves on a major issue. On top of this they had been long in power and the unexpectedly protracted mopping-up phase of the South African War had been a bitter disappointment to the country. A defeat was not surprising and it proved a major one. The Liberals came back 379 strong, and (a portent for the future) allied with them were 51 Labour Members. Conservative and Liberal Unionists together numbered only 157. "We have buried the Tories." The triumphant words were on many lips again as they had been in 1833. But the Tories were once again to survive and it was for the Liberal Party, now at the zenith of its power, that the sexton was soon to be called out.

BETWEEN THE WARS

At the outbreak of the First World War the Conservative Party assured Mr. Asquith's Liberal Government of their full support in all measures necessary for the defeat of the enemy. In 1915 they entered a Coalition Government which they supported until 1922, when the Party, led to this course by Baldwin, broke with Lloyd George, mainly because of his unpredictability in foreign affairs. Apart from two short periods when the Labour Party were in office, though in a minority in Parliament, the Conservative Party either alone or as the predominant partner in Coalition Governments were subsequently in power until the General Election of 1945.

Labour's second term of office, from 1929 to 1931, had one permanent effect on party alignment. The Socialist Party had claimed that they alone "had a positive remedy for unemployment," but (and here they were genuinely unlucky) their term of office coincided with the great American slump. Unemployment rose from 1,100,000 to 2,700,000 and Ministers, far from producing a positive and effective remedy, disagreed among themselves, did nothing, dithered and fell. At the General Election of 1931 only 56 Socialists were returned. The National Government which was formed to clean up the mess included the Liberals and a few Labour Members. When Protection and, in particular, measures to protect agriculture were introduced the Liberal Party split, the National Liberals remaining with the National Government and the Independent Liberals going into Opposition. The National Liberals—at present the larger wing of the Party in the House of Commons and probably in the country—are still allies of the Conservatives. This second swarming-off from the Liberal hive, though of less importance, was comparable to that of 1886.

Conservative politics during this time were dominated by Baldwin and Neville Chamberlain. Baldwin, in some ways a brilliant politician, believed with passion in the unity of the country, the wickedness of the class war and the need for mutual understanding in industry. It was due to him that neither the General Strike of 1926 nor the Abdication crisis left behind them the ugly scars that many predicted, and his toleration and good nature have not been without effect on the present generation of Socialist leaders.

In sharp contrast to Baldwin, Neville Chamberlain had all his father's radical individualism, reforming zeal and dislike of fools. As an adminis-

STANLEY BALDWIN ADDRESSING THE HOUSE DURING THE GENERAL STRIKE, 1926
Drawing by Stephen Spurrier from the *Illustrated London News*

trator and legislator he had much good work to his credit, including Contributory Widows', Orphans' and Old-Age Pensions, Holidays with Pay, Derating and Local-Government Reform, the cheap-money policy and a housing and slum-clearance drive which leaves the present Socialist Government panting behind. When he became Prime Minister he hoped and planned to concentrate on social and economic reform, which were his real interest in politics, but the shadow of Hitler fell across his path as the shadow of Napoleon had fallen across the path of the younger Pitt a hundred and fifty years before.

Neville Chamberlain had a horror of war—he was a passionate civilian. The First World War had shown the havoc that a total war fought by industrial nations could cause. The Second World War if it came would, he knew, be not only a war fought with the power and destructiveness of industrialism and democracy, but a religious war; and a religious war would mean that the restraints on the conduct of war which were a legacy from the eighteenth century would be abandoned and that the concluding phase of the second Thirty Years War would be waged as savagely as the first Thirty Years War had been waged in the seventeenth century. Chamberlain hated everything to do with the German National Socialist Party, its cruelty, its militarism and its denial of liberty; he thought Hitler half-mad; but with a full consciousness of what war would mean and a deep sense of his own responsibility, he could not bring himself to abandon hopes of peace. If war came there could be no prospect of easy victory. Germany, Italy and Japan were allied and had withdrawn from the League of Nations; America was not in the League of Nations and was unlikely to fight unless attacked; that Russia (though he did what he could to bring her into alliance) would prove treacherous Chamberlain rightly suspected, that the French Army was demoralised he half suspected; that in modern war the military value of small nations is negligible, he knew. At home the country was profoundly pacific and hardly stirred even under the lash of Mr. Churchill's oratory. The Socialists talked much of collective security, and collective security, if it meant anything, meant rearmament, but at the same time they were doing everything in their power to make rearmament politically impossible, even going so far as to vote against conscription after the rape of Prague in 1939. In verbal defiance they were prodigal. The typical attitude of the Socialist intellectual—vapid defiance before the war began and cold feet afterwards—was denounced towards the end of 1939 by the late Lord Keynes in the pages of the *New Statesman* in a letter of terrific scorn.

Neville Chamberlain was wrong in thinking that any accommodation was possible with Germany unless the balance of force was in our favour, as Mr. Bevin has been unsuccessful for the same reasons in his dealings with Russia, but he was less wrong than many of his critics (both wise and brave after the event) supposed.

The dust of the conflict which divided the Party on foreign policy before the war has not yet settled and, though the writer was bitterly opposed to Mr. Chamberlain's policy at the time, it may be that it is too early for a final judgment. But some things can be affirmed with confidence. Both wings of the Conservative Party were wiser than their Socialist opponents. The country entered the war united, an impossibility at the

NEVILLE CHAMBERLAIN AS CHANCELLOR OF THE EXCHEQUER
Oil painting by Oswald Birley, 1923

time of Munich; in 1939 our Navy was prepared and in 1940 our fighters had the numbers and the technical superiority to win the Battle of Britain. These were the essentials of victory.

Mr. Churchill became Prime Minister in 1940 at the crisis of the war and formed an all-party Government. Of his services to his country in winning the war it would be presumption to speak. His glory can never be tarnished. While fighting a desperate war much good work was done in preparing for the peace. Mr. R. A. Butler's Education Act had been passed in 1944, the Family Allowances Act in 1945, and the foundation had been laid for the rest of the subsequent reforms in the field of national insurance. Many expected Mr. Churchill's services to his country would gain him victory in the election of 1945, but strong forces were working against him. The political truce had been loyally observed by the Party, candidates and agents were on war work and constituency organisations had in most cases ceased to exist; the output of Party literature had been negligible at a time when Mr. Gollancz was selling his yellow-covered books of Socialist propaganda by the hundred thousand; personal losses and sufferings had been great, and these are generally blamed on the Government in power; two world wars had broken the "cake of custom"; and last, but not least, Socialist propaganda to the Forces, legitimate and illegitimate, had been powerful and continuous. Mr. Churchill, with the laurels of victory green upon his brow, went down to defeat and the Socialists gained a resounding victory. "We have buried the Tories." The voices were more strident and more confident than they had been in 1833 and 1906. But for whom would the sexton be called out?

CONSERVATIVE ELECTION POSTER, 1945
Issued by the Conservative and Unionist Party

PART II

CONSERVATIVE IDEAS AND CONSERVATIVE PEOPLE

PRINCIPLES

TO the question asked at the end of Part I we shall later return. The purpose of this section is to discuss the ideas which have animated and do animate the Party and which Tories during their long history have tried with varying success to carry out. Disraeli defined the principles of Conservatism in 1872:

> To maintain the institutions of the country.
> To uphold the Empire.
> To elevate the condition of the people.

To maintain, to uphold and to elevate; the static and the dynamic elements are both there. The static, because unless there is agreement on fundamentals and a determination to conserve the essentials of the constitution and the rule of Law, neither unity, safety nor strength is possible. As Lecky put it: "Institutions, like trees, can never attain their maturity or produce their proper fruits if their roots are being perpetually tampered with." The dynamic, because change is the law of life. As Burke put it, "Nothing in progression can rest on its original plan. We may as well think of rocking a grown man in the cradle of an infant." The task of Conservatism is therefore continually to transpose its care for social continuity into a contemporary key. In carrying out reforms it is their part never to be guilty of the apathetic fallacy of looking on people as abstractions, never to forget that, as Aristotle wrote, "Society was formed in order that men might live and is continued in order that they may live well." But men cannot live well to-day unless we hold on to the fundamentals; they cannot perhaps live at all unless somehow or other our old Christian tradition, our humanism and the culture we have inherited from Greece and Rome reassert their mastery in a world increasingly menaced with destruction by its own technical inventions. The first task then is to conserve the essentials and the second to carry out with good sense and humanity the reforms which time and changing circumstances make necessary.

Society, as the Conservative sees it, is a living body, an organism and not a mere convenience, contract or device; to quote Burke again, "It is a partnership in all science; a partnership in all art; a partnership in every virtue, and in all perfection. As the end of such a partnership cannot be obtained in many generations, it becomes a partnership not only between those who are living, but between those who are living, those who are dead, and those who are to be born." This conception of fundamental national unity in time, the conception that our ultimate identity of interest, our common experiences, the dangers we have faced and must face again together are of infinitely more importance than the differences that divide us, is the exact opposite of the Marxist conception of the class war. Mr. Bevan's savage boast, "We are going to see the right people squeal for a change," or Mr. Shinwell's belief that anyone who does not pay the political levy does not matter a tinker's curse, are sound Marxism, but anathema to a Conservative, who could never rejoice in the sufferings of any class or body of citizens any more than he could rejoice if he crushed his own thumb with a hammer. This does not mean that the existence of injustice or the obligation to remedy injustice is denied but that our ultimate unity is fundamental and perpetual while our differences are temporary and removable. Bound up with the idea of the State as a living body existing in time is the idea that the statesmen of the day hold the nation's possessions in trust for those that come after and that the dissipation of those possessions for a temporary political object, a dissipation which is now going on, is a sin against the nation.

A belief in the doctrine of original sin and a knowledge and understanding of history are both apt to make a man a Conservative. A belief in original sin is the basis of tolerance, mercy, moderation and good sense. It is a theological doctrine which is in full accord with the teaching of modern psychologists. The idea of perfectibility, the idea that if only there were no priests or if only there was absolute *laissez-faire* or Communism or democratic Socialism, then all the ills that men inherit would disappear leads inevitably to intolerance and the use of force. As Aldous Huxley put it: "Historically, progressiveness has always been associated with aggressiveness and the potentiality of greater good with the actuality of greater evil." The English Civil War, the French Revolution, and the Russian Revolution will serve as examples. Many Socialists believed against all the evidence of history that the German working classes would never follow Hitler in an aggressive war, and when they followed him blindly, the same men who had believed in their essential goodness were leading advocates of the use of the most ruthless weapons against them. Many more Socialists believed that with the imposition of "democratic" Socialism, the ordinary motives of economic conduct would be so weakened that, though the Law (in the form of statutory rules and orders) and legitimate self-interest were pulling in opposite directions, the rules and orders would be willingly obeyed. When the rules and orders were disobeyed there were cries of sabotage and conspiracy and calls for punishments, imprisonments and confiscations.

The idea of perfectibility is generally combined with a belief that some man or body of men knows exactly how a state of perfection can be brought about and that it is the duty of all other men to fall in with the perfectionist plan. The lesson of history is that while the decay and break-up of a civilisation and the return to barbarism are easy to bring about and can happen

HERBERT MORRISON LEADS THE ATTACK ON PRIVATE ENTERPRISE
Cartoon by Illingworth from *Punch*, November 28th, 1945

quickly even in an advanced society, just as the most polished iron rusts the quickest, progress, the ascent from a lower state of civilisation to a higher state of civilisation, must always be slow and difficult and that each step gained must be carefully consolidated. Violent changes lead to violence and to decay. Continuity is of the essence of the movement of growth.

"I had a State to preserve as well as a State to reform," said Burke. It is this sense of how much easier it is to do lasting harm than lasting good that makes the Conservative a cautious reformer. He knows that the attempt to break away from the present and jump into another reach of the time stream is a forlorn hope. He is sceptical of the divine inspiration of the spirit of the age, he knows that the *zeitgeist* is just as likely to be a spirit of evil as a spirit of good. The onus of proof, he believes, lies on the innovator.

33

No Conservative would have preached nationalisation as a cure-all for fifty years and then been forced to confess, as Mr. Shinwell so honestly did, that he and his party had never thought deeply upon the problems involved. This distrust of the plenary inspiration of the *zeitgeist*, this refusal to believe that because our fathers were fools we are necessarily wise men, this disbelief in short cuts and simple answers is fundamental to Conservatism. Conservatism seeks to get out of every fresh development, each new line of thought, what is of value, but to prevent enthusiasm for the fashionable cure of the day leading to a state of unbalance which may do lasting damage to the country. Thus Tories stood against Charles I in the early stages of the constitutional crisis and fought for him in the later stages; thus they took an active part in liberalising our economy in the early part of the nineteenth century when it was encumbered by a tariff structure of great complexity, and still tied down by Tudor legislation, and took their stand against *laissez-faire* and for authority in the later years of the same century; and thus to-day they are seeking to preserve what was of lasting value in nineteenth-century Liberalism against the ever-increasing aggression of an authoritarian State.

REACTION

If you are sceptical about the spirit of the age, if you accord less than full belief to whatever the current nonsense happens to be, you are sure to be dubbed both stupid and reactionary. It may be that stupidity is the characteristic vice of the Right, just as folly is the characteristic vice of the Left (it is an arguable proposition), but "reaction" used as a term of abuse causes such confusion of thought that some discussion of the word may be useful. The virtues or vices of reaction depend upon what it is that you are reacting against. If you stick a large pin into a man's body and get no reaction you may reasonably conclude, not that he is in the van of progress, but that he is either dead, paralysed or drunk. Conservatives were right to react against the doctrine of *laissez-faire* when they passed the Ten Hours Bill in 1847, as they are right to-day to react against an authoritarian economy. And Conservatives who are in a state of permanent reaction against the characteristic types of the Left are in company with the immortals. As M. André Suarès (quoted by Maurice Baring in *Have you Anything to Declare?*) has it: "Tous les grands poètes, sans aucune exception, si ce n'est au dix-neuvième siècle, ont été réactionnaires comme on dit, également ennemis des tribuns et des pédants. C'est un fait, et on n'y peut rien. Les textes sont là, d'Homère à Baudelaire, de la Genese à Goethe, d'Aristophane à Cervantes et d'Eschyle à Shakespeare." The texts are there and so are the tribunes and the pedants, more numerous, more strident and more foolish than ever. That they should provoke no reaction would be a disgrace.

A FREE-TRADE FORECAST

Victorian poster designed and printed by Percival Jones Ltd, Birmingham
Issued by the Imperial Tariff Committee, Birmingham

It is their acute sense of the fallibility of human judgment, the lesson they have gained from history that no set of human beings ever knows all the answers and that those who believe that they have an infallible answer are always potential persecutors, that has always made Conservatives so distrustful of the concentration of power. They do not believe that the present type of central planning, which involves the attempt by the State to interfere in almost every aspect of human life and activity, can succeed or if it did succeed would lead to the good life. As a distinguished economist, Mr. Cairncross, says of the conception of the direction of economic planning by some benevolent master mind at the centre, "The plain fact is that master minds capable of such direction do not exist; or if they do, they are not at the centre; or if they are, they are not benevolent or not benevolent for long." Nor if such planners could be conceived as always benevolent is the objection removed, for, to quote a Conservative sentiment from Mr. Aldous Huxley again, "It is probable that plans, made by well-meaning people of the second class, may have results no less disastrous than plans made by evil-intentioned people of the first class." The present Socialist authoritarian economy, combined as it is with the power and patronage that nationalisation puts in the hands of authority, is an extreme example of the concentration of power. Conservatives have opposed much lesser examples, such as the Venetian Oligarchy of the Whigs in the eighteenth century, the rising moneyed interest in the City in the eighteenth and nineteenth centuries, the power of the radical manufacturers in the nineteenth century, and the Venetian Oligarchy at Transport House in the twentieth century. The present dangers call for still stouter resistance.

This distrust of the concentration of power and sectional control would in any case make Conservatives oppose nationalisation and an authoritarian economy; but there are two other vital considerations which influence them. An authoritarian economy is bound to lead to direction of labour (or more simply put, to slavery) and to the loss of consumer's choice, and it is bound to lead to inefficiency. Ministers, and Mr. Attlee in particular, were deeply sworn against the direction of labour, but the remorseless logic of Socialism, which has surprised only them, has forced them to adopt it. The loss of consumer's choice, the allotment of so many goods on the basis of coupon and permit, will amount in the long run to the reimposition of truck payments on a vast scale and a decisive weakening both of incentive and the pleasure derived even by the poorest in laying out their income to the best advantage. It leads to endless absurdities. To-day you can buy imported nuts but not imported butter, imported champagne but not imported petrol.

As regards the effect of centralisation on efficiency, Keynes in his *General Theory* has this comment: "The advantage to efficiency of the decentralisation of decisions and of individual responsibility is even greater perhaps than the nineteenth century supposed; and the reaction against the appeal to self-interest may have gone too far." The Tories fought in the nineteenth century against the right of Liberal manufacturers to do exactly as they liked with their own; Disraeli and the Young England group constantly upheld the truth that property has duties as well as rights; Tories have never believed that the profit motive was an entire and sufficient motive for economic conduct. But to-day, under Socialism, the reaction against reliance on purely economic motives has gone too far, the position is out of balance. After all, there is more sense in the profit motive than the loss motive, and to buy cheap and sell dear is better than to buy dear and sell cheap as bulk purchasers so often do. In a hard world the race will not always be to the slow.

CONSERVATIVE PEOPLE

What sort of people support the Conservative Party? The answer is, the most diverse sorts of people. A party without a rigid orthodoxy, a party not given to heresy-hunting, has room for all sorts and conditions of men and women. It contains many types of Tory from the high-and-dry to the extreme Tory democrat; it contains many hundreds of thousands of Liberals who see that in the present age it is the Tories who are the guardians and preservers of the nineteenth-century gains of Liberalism which the Socialist Party is bent on destroying and which the Liberal Party itself no longer has the power to uphold; it contains many who are simply anti-Socialist; and lastly, it contains the contented of all classes; if you meet anyone of whatever class who is continually sweating and whining about his condition, anyone who has an exceptionally good face for a grievance, you may be sure that he is on the Left.

That the Conservative Party is a class party is a jibe at least a hundred and fifty years old. The first thing one is tempted to ask any Socialist who puts forward this view is "What then is all the fuss about?" A party composed exclusively of the rich and great would have had no chance at the polls since 1867. Anyone actively engaged in Conservative politics knows from his own experience that his supporters come from all classes, and the results of a Gallup Poll conducted early in 1948 gave interesting statistical confirmation of this. Those questioned were asked to what class they belonged. 36 per cent. said upper, upper middle or middle and 59 per cent. said lower middle or working class. Of the first group, that is to say those who classed themselves as middle to upper class, 24 per cent. voted Labour at the last election; of the second group, the lower-middle and working-class group, 23 per cent. declared that they would vote Conservative at the next election. The figures show both the diversity of our class structure (a fact existing in Marx's day but ignored by him) and that the line of political division in this country is oblique and not horizontal.

THE OLD-FASHIONED TORY
Cartoon by Sir Max Beerbohm

A Conservative, then, is a man who holds fast to certain fundamental beliefs: to a belief in the religious basis of society, to a belief in our monarchical constitution, to a belief in the institution of private property, to a belief in the ancient virtues of patriotism, honesty, hard work and tolerance, to a belief in the authority attaching to the work of Time. Without these beliefs nations lose their essential cohesion and revert all too easily to barbarism. Combined with these fundamental beliefs is a scepticism about easy cures or solutions of the human dilemma, a refusal to worship fashionable idols—a refusal to bow in the house of Rimmon—and a determination to apply to the problems of the day an opportunism which is modified and controlled by principle, by respect for history, by good sense and by good manners.

MR. ANTHONY EDEN IN THE HOUSE OF COMMONS
Cartoon by J. Ross, 1947

38

PART III

THE PARTY SINCE THE ELECTION OF 1945

THE results of the General Election of 1945 presented the Conservative Party with a challenge. Numbers were low in the House of Commons, constituency organisation was almost non-existent, finances were exhausted, Party literature weak, our opponents were in the seventh heaven of triumph and exultation and there was a tendency in the country to turn from the Tories in order to greet the rising sun of Socialism. It looked wise at the time and there would be jobs about. The challenge has proved to be of exactly the right strength to produce the maximum response—had it been stronger, discouragement might have been too great to be healthy; had it been weaker the Party would not have had the shaking-up it needed. The result of the election was deeply disappointing but it was not altogether surprising, and Tories had been too long in the game to be cast down over-much by a beating at the polls. The Party was not divided as it had been in 1714 and numbers were greater than they had been in 1833 or 1906. What was needed was hard thinking about the place of the Party in the post-war world, a restatement of policy as in 1833 and another such reorganisation of the Party machine as had taken place after previous defeats.

In foreign affairs no formal written restatement of policy was issued, but Mr. Churchill in his Fulton speech drew the attention of the world to the dangers of Russian expansion and by organising the United Europe movement did as much as any man in a private station could do to provide the remedy. In the House of Commons the Party continually hammered the Government for the moral wrongs and the practical ineptitude of their policy in the key area of Western Germany. The criticism has not been without effect and slowly but surely the Government are following the Conservative lead, though always clumsily and always two years late.

It was on industrial, agricultural and Imperial policy that formal statements of policy were issued. Unlike the Tamworth Manifesto, the Conservative Industrial Charter was not an election programme, nor was it a restatement of principles such as has recently been brilliantly done by Mr. Quintin Hogg in his *Case for Conservatism*, nor was it simple propaganda. It was, first, an examination on an intellectual level much above the ordinary run of party political literature of the question posed by Alfred Marshall as central to economics, "How shall we act so as to increase the good and diminish the evil influence of economic freedom?" or, to put it another way, in the post-war world what are the precise limits of judicious State intervention for a party pledged to maintain a high and stable level of employment? And secondly, what could and should be done to further the cause of better human relations in industry? The authors of the Charter,

39

led by Mr. R. A. Butler (a student of the life of Peel), writing before the fuel crisis in early 1947 started by pointing out that the inevitable consequence of Daltonian finance would be a balance-of-payments crisis. This, in view of subsequent events, may look like a blinding glimpse of the obvious, but it was a shock to the country at a time when Ministers were vying with each other in describing the glories of the Golden Age to come. The second part of the Charter dealt with the crucial question of the place of Government in a free society. The Charter accepted as a prime object of policy the duty of the Government to ensure a high and stable level of employment and in effect accepted the views of Lord Keynes (a moderately conservative reformer) on the cause and cure of unemployment. The general direction of our economy was to be exercised through the Budget, through monetary policy and through the control, whether direct or indirect, of capital expenditure. One Minister was to be responsible for surveying the whole of our national resources—a method since adopted by the Government. Such central controls (correctly administered so as to avoid either inflation or deflation) would make unnecessary the bulk of detailed controls over the operations of industry which now hold back production. The policy was therefore the precise opposite of that so far pursued by the Socialist Government. In the words of the Charter "We wish to substitute for the present paralysis, in which we are experiencing the worst of all worlds, a system of free enterprise, which is on terms with authority, and which reconciles the need for central direction with the encouragement of individual effort."

It was recognised as essential to our recovery and essential if a policy of abundance was to be substituted for the present policy of restriction that there should be the greatest possible degree of decentralisation of decision and the greatest stimulus to individual effort. Individual effort would not be stimulated unless there was both incentive and competition. The authors of the Charter accepted the truth of Marshall's saying, "Progress mainly depends on the extent to which the strongest and not merely the highest forces of human nature can be utilised for the increase of social good." If incentives were to be stronger there must be lower Government expenditure, leading to lower taxation, and a reform of the incidence of P.A.Y.E.; measures to deal with monopoly (since adopted by the Government) were suggested in order to stimulate competition.

The third part of the Charter—the workers' charter—started with the essentially Tory words "Our policy is to humanise, not to nationalise. Human relations are of first importance in industry. We do not agree with any view of industry which divides those engaged in it into 'sides' with mutually opposed interests. If the sum of human welfare and happiness is to be increased in this country, it will be only through fostering a sense of united purpose among all those engaged in industry whatever their position." Nationalisation has clearly not given to workers any increased

THE HOUSE OF COMMONS: THE TORIES IN OPPOSITION
Detail from a crayon drawing by J. Ross, 1947

feelings of interest, personal contact or united purpose—rather the reverse. The object must be to bring back into large-scale industry the personal contact and interest most easily found in the small firm, and to raise the standard of welfare services of small firms to that more often found in large firms. Many approaches to a better state of affairs were suggested: greater security, longer contracts of service; payments by results, opportunity for promotion and future education and training, joint consultation and, where applicable, co-partnership and, above all, unity and good feeling. These are not things for which it is easy to legislate, but the ingenious suggestion was made that a code of labour relations should be drawn up and given Parliamentary approval on the analogy of a Fair Wages Clause and that in due course the provisions of the code should be enforced. The Charter was approved by the Tory Conference with only three dissentients and its doctrine has been actively propagated.

The Party believe in private property as necessary for liberty, happiness and stability. On Burke's principle that what comprehends most is most secure they are therefore anxious for the greatest possible diffusion of ownership. This aspect of policy, which was not dealt with at length in the Charter, has been taken up especially by Mr. Eden and the present Lord Salisbury who have taken the lead in preaching the ideal of a property-owning democracy.

They have put forward the conception of a democracy where the essentials of life are secured to all, a democracy where not only property but also power is diffused to the greatest possible extent and a democracy where talent is rewarded and all have their part to play in the National Community.

The Agricultural Charter recognised the vastly increased importance of domestic food production to a Britain now, as a result of the Second World War, without the means to pay for food imports and without reserves. The wheel has come full circle since 1846—Disraeli has triumphed over Peel and the necessary measures to give those who get their living by the land their rightful place in the State can at last be taken.

The Charter sets out the rights and duties of landlords, farmers and farmworkers and suggests many improvements on the system of control worked out during the war.

PARTY ORGANISATION

The constitution of the Conservative Party symbolises the Tory ideal of leadership by consent. The leader is elected by and removable by a body consisting of the Parliamentary Party, the adopted candidates and the Executive Committee of the National Union of Constituency Associations. Once elected, and so long as he retains the confidence of the electing body,

By courtesy of the Rt. Hon. Winston Churchill and the Artist

THE RT. HON. WINSTON CHURCHILL
AFTER BROADCASTING AN ELECTION SPEECH, JUNE 1945
Oil sketch by Major John Churchill, 1946

the leader is responsible for the policy of the party; he appoints the Chairman of the Party, and through him the principal officers of the Conservative Central Office. Whilst, therefore, the leader is ultimately responsible to the Constituency Associations, he himself directly controls the Central Office and with it the Research Department and other policy-forming committees, the dissemination of party literature and the party purse.

The Constituency Associations are grouped into twelve areas in England and Wales and there are separate organisations for Scotland and Ulster, but the pith and strength of the party is in the individual Constituency Association itself. Every subscriber (the minimum subscription is settled by each Association individually and ranges from 1s. per annum upwards) has the right to vote for the election of officers for his ward or polling-district committee and for the election of officers of his Constituency Association and the selection of a candidate. Members are gained by house-to-house canvassing, by public meetings, by social events and by the distribution of party literature (five times as great in 1947 as in 1946). New members have been recruited in large numbers; by the spring of 1948 over a million had already subscribed, and a campaign to get a second million was successfully concluded during the summer. All members are true volunteers who join as individuals, whereas in the case of the Socialist Party the bulk of the membership comes from trade-unionists who have not contracted out of the political levy, and the individual membership of the Socialist Party (608,000 in 1947) actually decreased by 37,000 on the year. More energy than ever before is being shown by Conservatives and the cause is everywhere preached from the mountains of Wales to the East End of London.

As well as gaining members, a Constituency Association must collect money, send representatives to the Annual Party Conference and, if there is no sitting Member, select a candidate. The objective in constituency finance is that an Association shall be self-supporting both as regards current expenses and for the purpose of fighting an election. Not only has this objective been attained in the majority of constituencies but large sums were subscribed by Constituency Associations to Lord Woolton's £1,000,000 fighting fund. Attendance at the Party Conference is twice as high as before the war and the proceedings have never been conducted with greater vigour and political knowledge.

Constituencies are jealous of their rights in selecting candidates and as they are mostly independent financially they are in a strong position to resent any attempt at dictation by the Central Office. It is open to the Socialist Party managers to select the by-election candidate they think most suitable. They can weigh the relative appeal of a baronet or the younger son of a peer for a suburban seat; but any attempt by the Conservative Central Office to set aside the candidate selected by the local Association would be more than likely to fail. No candidate is permitted to subscribe to his

43

association more than £100 a year and half his election expenses. More than half the selected candidates pay either less than the maximum or nothing at all. Candidates are drawn from many walks of life (a solvent Association has a free choice) and one-half of those adopted received their education through the Secondary School system. Few constituencies have not yet adopted candidates, and there is a long waiting list.

The Young Conservative Movement—which all Conservatives between 15 and 30 years of age can join—has made great strides; in 1948 there were in the United Kingdom about 2,000 branches and nearly 150,000 members. The movement is not simply out for education and social amusement (though both these aspects are important), it is for use. Young Conservatives are represented by their own members on all constituency executive committees, at the Party Conference and on the central policy and education committee of the Party, and they have made their voices heard. They have given help by speaking and canvassing at by-elections and local government elections; a number of Young Conservatives have won seats at Council elections and a number will be candidates at the coming General Election. The movement represents an avenue of political advancement for an able young man or woman.

The two-way movement of ideas, an innovation started by the Conservative Education Movement, promises to be of some importance in the future. Factual pamphlets on the questions of the day are circulated to discussion groups working on the A.B.C.A. principle. The discussion groups, of which about 650 were at work at the beginning of 1948, draw up a report of their findings and opinions which is then sent up by way of area headquarters to the Conservative Political Centre. The reports are analysed and the results are then set out in a pamphlet which comes out twice each year and is widely circulated in the Party. The two-way movement of ideas therefore serves not only to educate members of the Party but to keep the leaders in touch with opinion among active rank-and-file Conservatives in the constituencies and to ventilate new ideas.

There are many other activities such as film production, book shops, Conservative clubs, Trade Union advisory committees, weekend schools, a new residential college and so forth, of which there is not space to write. But one last point must be made. In all work for the Party women are prominent. In an industrial society men tend to lead a highly specialised and artificial life, whereas women who bear the children and cook the food do not lose touch with the fundamental realities. They are less easily persuaded by pure nonsense than men and a higher proportion of them are therefore Conservatives. Since the Election, progress by the Party in all its activities has been encouraging. There is no shortage of ideas or workers or subscribers, reorganisation progresses, and apathy is now a Socialist disease. The Party is full of life. To the Conservative Party at any rate the sexton will not be called out.

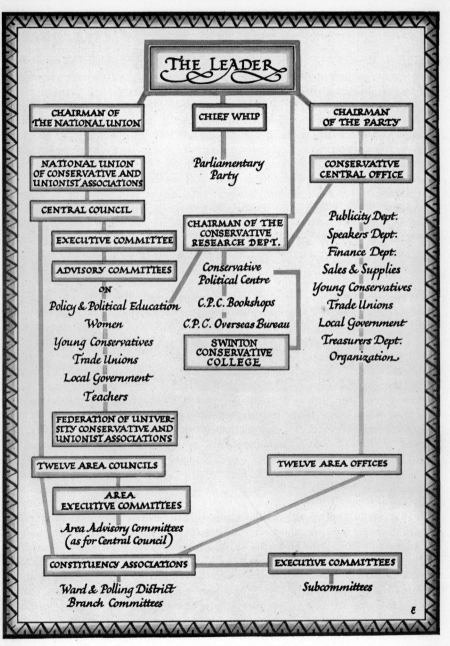

THE LEADER

| CHAIRMAN OF THE NATIONAL UNION | CHIEF WHIP | CHAIRMAN OF THE PARTY |

NATIONAL UNION OF CONSERVATIVE AND UNIONIST ASSOCIATIONS

Parliamentary Party

CONSERVATIVE CENTRAL OFFICE

CENTRAL COUNCIL

EXECUTIVE COMMITTEE

CHAIRMAN OF THE CONSERVATIVE RESEARCH DEPT.

Publicity Dept.
Speakers Dept.
Finance Dept.

ADVISORY COMMITTEES

ON

Policy & Political Education
Women
Young Conservatives
Trade Unions
Local Government
Teachers

Conservative Political Centre

C.P.C. Bookshops

C.P.C. Overseas Bureau

SWINTON CONSERVATIVE COLLEGE

Sales & Supplies
Young Conservatives
Trade Unions
Local Government
Treasurers Dept.
Organization

FEDERATION OF UNIVERSITY CONSERVATIVE AND UNIONIST ASSOCIATIONS

TWELVE AREA COUNCILS

TWELVE AREA OFFICES

AREA EXECUTIVE COMMITTEES

Area Advisory Committees (as for Central Council)

CONSTITUENCY ASSOCIATIONS

EXECUTIVE COMMITTEES

Ward & Polling District Branch Committees

Subcommittees

E

CHART OF THE CONSERVATIVE PARTY ORGANISATION

PART IV

THE FUTURE

IN 1949 it is not difficult to see the dangers with which Britain is faced. There is first the danger of aggressive Russian Communism in a Europe where no balance of power exists, a danger to peace, to our values, our way of life and our liberties and a danger to our standard of living. And secondly, there is the danger not only to our standard of living but perhaps also to our national character presented by our balance-of-payments difficulties—by our present inability to pay for vital food and raw material imports. For this country not to be able to pay for the food she needs is a break in the continuity of our history as sharp as the Norman Conquest. How much our national character is due to the wealth, ease, security and power we have enjoyed in the past we have still to learn. How do the political parties face up to these challenges?

LIBERALS

Our electoral system would in any case prevent Mr. Clement Davies's wing of the Liberal Party playing much part in the struggle even if party leadership and party ability to re-think and re-state their position in the world to-day were stronger than they are.

Liberals in isolation can give no answer to the challenge. On the periphery, in the constituencies, there is a tendency for alliances between Liberals and Conservatives to be formed—when they get together they find it difficult with the best will in the world to find anything of importance to disagree about—but there is little or no likelihood of the Old Guard who control what is left of the party machine ever becoming firm allies of the Tories. Their hopes and their memories are of distant days before Socialism grew to power, when the Tories were the only and much hated enemies.

SOCIALISTS

It has recently become the fashion among Socialists to say that their party represents the only "democratic" alternative to Communism. In order to rally the faithful, Mr. Herbert Morrison tells them that the Communist Party is not, as they had supposed, on the Left, but on the Right (students of *Mein Kampf* will recognise the technique) and Mr. Attlee assures them that his ideas do not represent a temporary halting-place between Capitalism and Communism but a permanent way of life. Opposition to Communism is not something on which the Socialist Party is entirely united; this is not surprising, for the conversion has been quick. As late as 1944 Mr. Harold Laski (re-elected to the party executive in 1948) was writing

46

BANNER OF THE PRIMROSE LEAGUE
The League was founded in 1883 in memory of Disraeli and to perpetuate his principles

in his *Faith, Reason and Civilisation*, "Unless we claim that the Churches will renew their hold on men's allegiance—and there is no serious evidence for the validity of such a claim—the Russian idea seems likely to be the pivotal source from which all values will find the means of renewal. . . . We were aware that a new world-outlook was in making in Russia; but we could not come to terms with it unless we recognised how profound were the changes we must accept in our own philosophy of value. It is this refusal to come to terms with the Russian faith that is perhaps the source of the greatest danger we confront to-day on the moral plane." Nor is it easy to believe that Mr. Attlee's democratic Socialism is more than a "temporary halting-place," for it is essentially self-contradictory, an attempt to set up an authoritarian economy without the use of force. Either you must go back to freedom or you must use more force. So far the movement has been towards a greater use of force; direction of labour has been introduced and penalties for black-market building imposed equal to those for perjury and incest. Who can doubt that sterner measures would have been used if pre-Socialist traditions were not still so strong? Stalin does not claim that Russia is a Communist State, he claims that it is a Socialist State; Socialism and water can hardly be the answer to Socialism. It certainly has not been in Eastern Europe. Nor does the Socialist authoritarian economy look like providing the answer to our balance-of-payments difficulties which would without aid from capitalist America already have brought us to disaster. The rising costs and low production in the coal trade are a warning of what we may expect from nationalisation, and the confusion in our economy generally tends to increase. The division in the party between those who want more force and those who want less is beginning to widen. The Marxist wing of the party is much the same size as the whole party was in 1906. If the party does crack, it is a fair though a depressing prediction that it will be the right wing for whom the sexton will be called out.

CONSERVATIVES

We have seen in the Liberals an inability to deal with the dangers that face us and in the Socialists an absence of the will and faith that are needed. The Conservatives remain. They have the organisation, the strength, the faith and the courage which the hour demands. They are united and clear where they stand with regard to Russian Communism, they know that in the present age it is their task to defend the free society and they will not be guilty of what Professor Toynbee describes as that "cynical loss of faith in the recently established principles and a nerveless surrender of the recently won gains of liberalism, that have been perpetrated by our intellectuals within living memory." They know that the answer to slavery is not a milder form of slavery but freedom. They know that if Britain is to regain her position in world trade, if she is to compete with America, she will need to have American standards of efficiency and that these are not likely to be attained by wholesale collectivism but by a revived, reinvigorated and up-to-date capitalism. And they do not despair. Despair is too much in the fashion. M. Bertrand de Jouvenel wrote in his *Problème de l'Angleterre Socialiste* of the weakness of the West: "Pour quelques-uns comme Mr. Churchill c'est une angoisse vécue, pour d'autres une fatalité acceptée." We have lived through the agony, but we need not accept our weakness as a fatality. That our standard of life and the scope for individual choice and decision should diminish at a time when our command of productive power is greater than ever before is not something inevitably fated; it is the result, as Keynes said, of "an underlying contradiction in every department of our economy." This contradiction must be resolved. As a country we have been abundantly blessed in the past; the heart and spirit of the people are still sound and we have not lost our skill or brains. Our sun has not yet set.

CONSERVATIVE PEERS IN THE HOUSE OF LORDS
Detail from a cartoon by J. Ross, 1947

SHORT BIBLIOGRAPHY

All standard works on British History from the reign of Henry VIII
to the present day are relevant to the study of the Conservative Party.
The following works are specifically devoted to Conservative history
and ideas.

A History of the Tory Party, 1640-1714 by Keith Feiling. 1924, Oxford
University Press.—*The Second Tory Party, 1714-1832* by Keith Feiling.
1938, Macmillan.—*Lord Randolph Churchill* by Winston Churchill. 2 vols.
1906, Macmillan.—*The Life of Benjamin Disraeli, Earl of Beaconsfield*
by W. F. Monypenny and G. E. Buckle. 6 vols. 1910-1920, John Murray.
—*The Tory Tradition* by Geoffrey G. Butler. 1914, John Murray.—
Burke, a Historical Study by Lord Morley. 1925, Macmillan.—*Sir Robert
Peel* by A. A. W. Ramsay. 1928, Constable.—*The Life of Robert, Marquess
of Salisbury* by Lady Gwendolen Cecil. 4 vols. 1932, Hodder & Stoughton.
—*The Life of Joseph Chamberlain* by J. L. Garvin. 3 vols. 1932-1934,
Macmillan.—*Conservatism in England* by F. J. C. Hearnshaw. 1933,
Macmillan.—*The Life of Neville Chamberlain* by Keith Feiling. 1946,
Macmillan.—*The Case for Conservatism* by Quintin Hogg. 1947, Penguin
Books.—*Party Choice* by Michael Berry. 1948, Eyre & Spottiswoode